WEST BROAD STREET SCHOOL
131 WEST BROAD STREET
PAWCATUCK, CONNECTICUT
06379

A monarch butterfly settles on the leaf of a milkweed plant.

She gently presses a tiny egg on to one of its leaves.
The egg is the beginning of another . . .

MONARCH BUTTERFLY

BY GAIL GIBBONS

HOLIDAY HOUSE
NEW YORK

For Kate Briggs

Copyright © 1989 by Gail Gibbons
All rights reserved
Printed in the United States of America

Library of Congress Cataloging-in-Publication Data
Gibbons, Gail.
Monarch butterfly / written and illustrated by Gail Gibbons. —
1st ed.
p.   cm.
Summary: Describes the life cycle, body parts, and behavior of the
monarch butterfly. Includes instructions on how to raise a monarch.
ISBN 0-8234-0773-X
1. Monarch butterfly—Juvenile literature.   [1. Monarch
butterfly.   2. Butterflies.]   I. Title.
QL561.D3G53   1989
595.78'9—dc 19   89-1880   CIP   AC

ISBN 0-8234-0773-X
ISBN 0-8234-0909-0 (pbk.)

It's summertime in the north. A breeze stirs the stem
of the milkweed plant. The monarch egg is white and shiny.
It is the size of a small dot and sticks to the leaf.

When the butterfly lays the egg, she makes it sticky.
Wind and rain cannot make the egg come loose.

**CATERPILLAR
or LARVA**

In a few days the egg hatches. Out crawls a small caterpillar, also called a larva. First the caterpillar eats the eggshell and then chews away at the milkweed leaf. The egg of a monarch is almost always laid on a milkweed plant. The plant will be its food.

The caterpillar eats and grows and begins to change. It breaks out of its old skin, showing a new skin underneath. This is called molting.

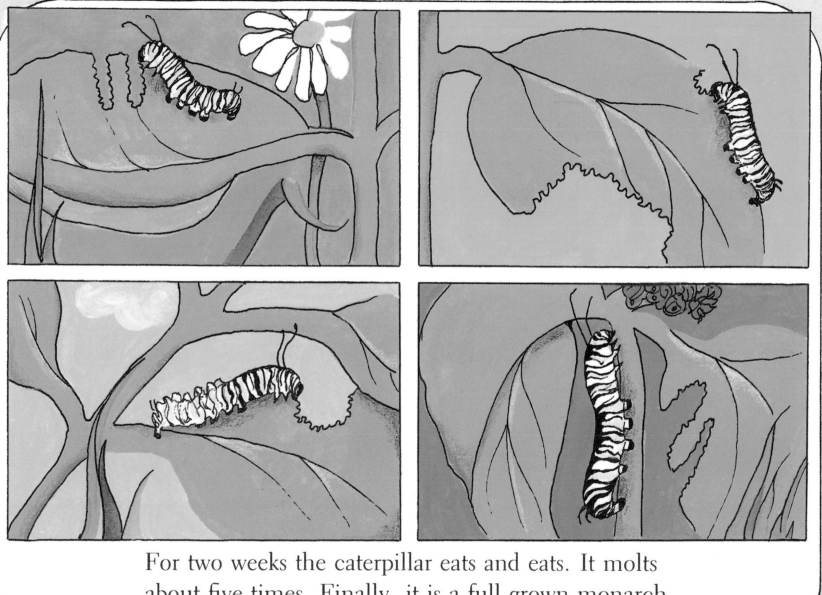

For two weeks the caterpillar eats and eats. It molts about five times. Finally, it is a full grown monarch caterpillar, about two inches long.

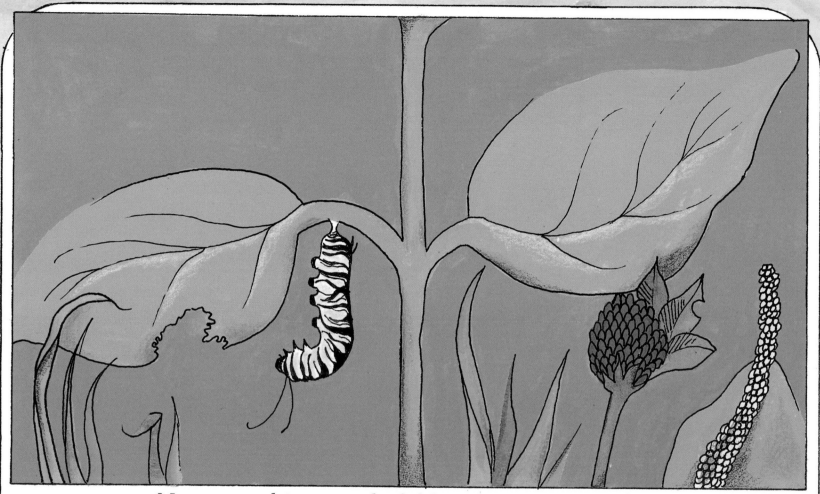

Now something wonderful begins to happen. The caterpillar creeps to the stem of a leaf. It attaches itself to the stem and drops down head first. The caterpillar's bright colors become greenish.

CHRYSALIS
KRISS-uh-liss
or
PUPA
PEW-pa

Then the skin splits and moves up to the top.
The skin falls off. A new, strange form appears!
It is called the chrysalis or pupa. The chrysalis
is like a blanket that is wrapped around the body
growing inside.

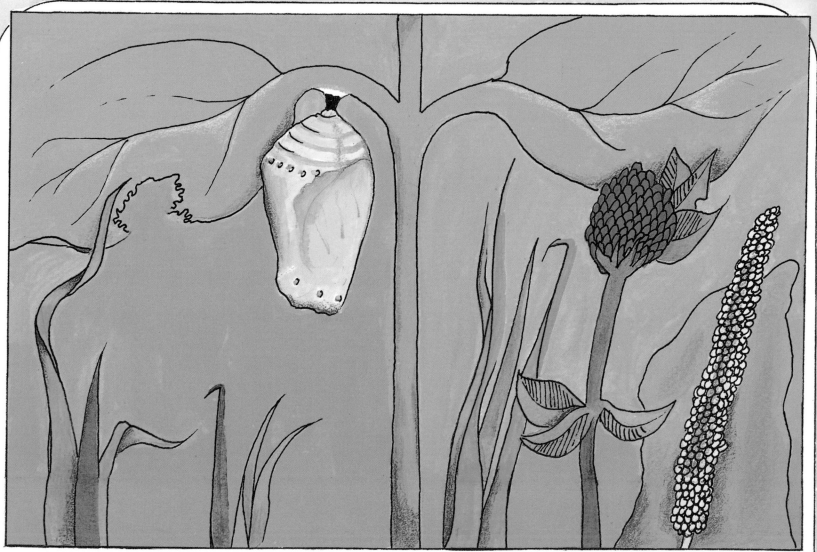

At first, the chrysalis is long and soft. Then it
shrinks and hardens, and becomes light green decorated
with gold dots. Inside, the monarch butterfly begins to grow.

About two weeks later, the chrysalis changes again.
It turns gray green before becoming transparent.
Inside are white dots, and orange and black lines.

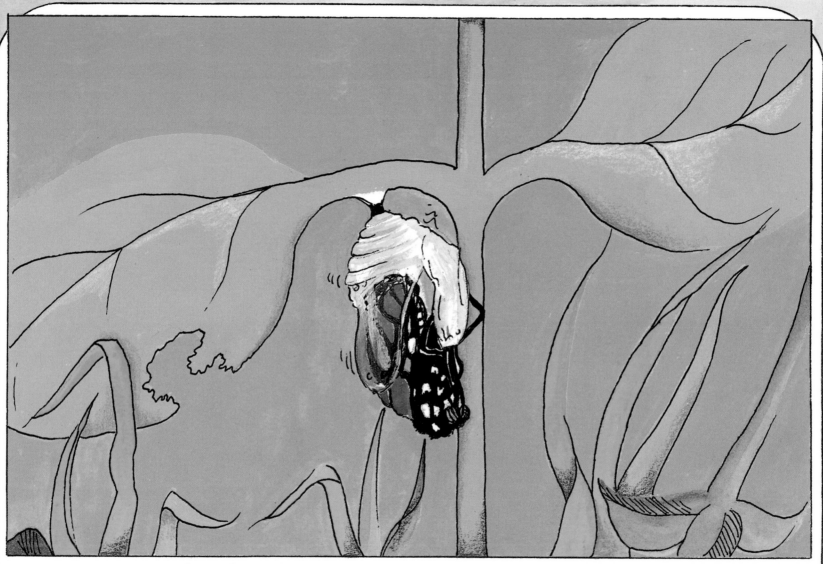

The chrysalis wiggles. Then it splits open. The butterfly begins to pull itself out. The head and legs appear first, and then the rest of it slides out.

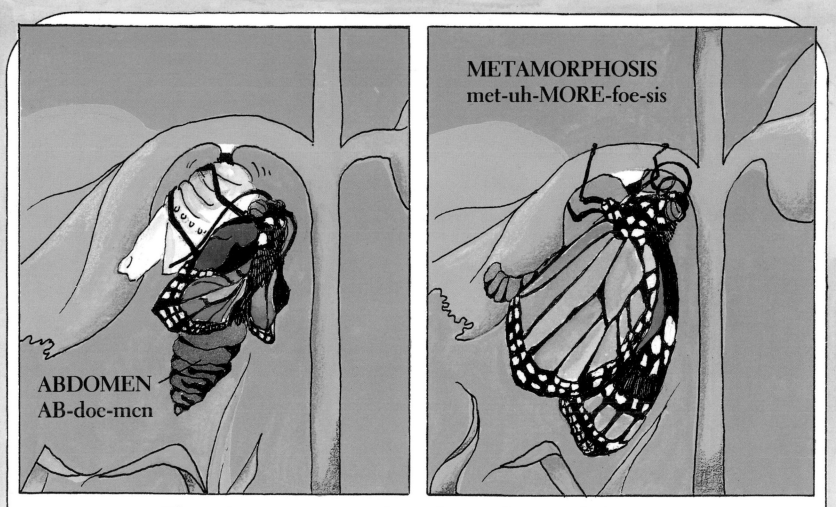

ABDOMEN
AB-doe-men

METAMORPHOSIS
met-uh-MORE-foe-sis

The wings are tiny and stuck together, and the butterfly's abdomen is big. The abdomen becomes smaller when its fluid is pumped into the wings. The wings become bigger. A caterpillar has turned into a butterfly. This is called metamorphosis.

The butterfly sits quietly for a few hours, waiting for its wings to dry and harden. At last they begin to move slowly, and then beat faster and faster.

The butterfly flutters up toward the sky. Monarchs
have a bad taste and will make a bird or animal
sick if they are eaten, so most of them are left alone.

The SCALES of the wings make up the colors.

SCALES

The FEELER or ANTENNA is for touch and smell.

FEELER or ANTENNA
an-TEN-a

HEAD

The tube to the mouth is called the PROBOSCIS. It sucks up sweet juice, called nectar, from flowers.

WING

PROBOSCIS
pro-BASS-is

THORAX
THOR-ax

ABDOMEN
AB-doe-men

LEG

There are many parts to a butterfly.

The monarch butterfly only flies during the day.
When it rains, the butterfly stays dry, hidden
under leaves.

Fall is on the way. Soon it will be cold. If the
monarch butterfly doesn't fly south, it will die.
Once again, it darts up into the sky.

The butterfly will take a long trip to a warmer place. This is called migration.

The monarch will fly to where its ancestors have always gone . . . sometimes to the very same tree!

Other monarchs keep appearing, making a cloud of
orange in the sky. At night they rest in trees.

Sometimes they fly up to 12 miles an hour and almost 100 miles in one day. There could be over 1,000 butterflies traveling together.

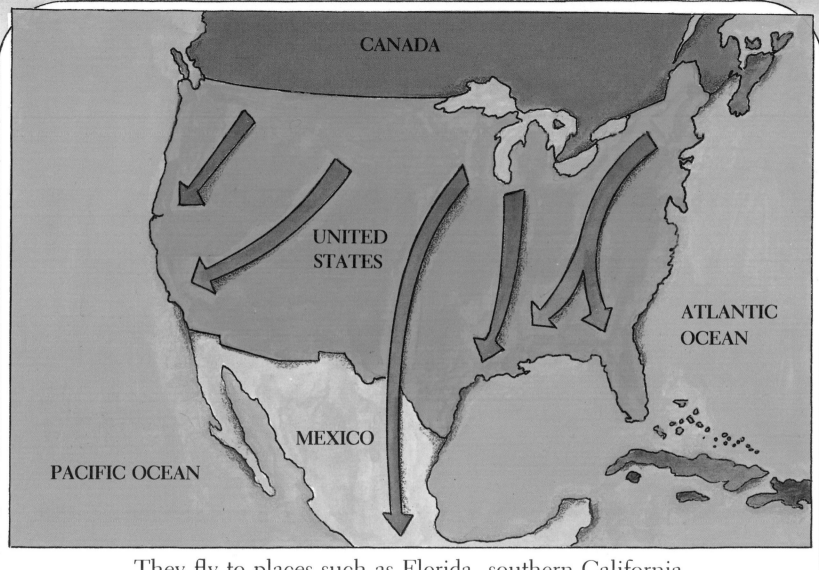

They fly to places such as Florida, southern California, and Mexico. Some butterflies migrate 4,000 miles! They will stay south throughout the winter.

Some towns and cities are proud to have the butterflies visit them. They have festivals to celebrate their arrival.

Children dress up for parades in butterfly costumes. Sometimes there's a band, and visitors come from all around.

Monarchs can cluster together, thousands of them
clinging to one tree. A butterfly tree!

In the spring these butterflies will migrate north
again to the fields of milkweed plants.

HOW TO RAISE A MONARCH BUTTERFLY

HOW TO MAKE A HOME FOR YOUR MONARCH CATERPILLAR

Find a big, clean glass jar with a metal lid. Pound several holes in the lid with a hammer and nail, so air can get inside the jar.

HOW TO FIND YOUR MONARCH CATERPILLAR

Late July and August is the best time to find a monarch caterpillar. Go to a field where milkweed plants grow. Look underneath the milkweed leaves. When you find a monarch caterpillar, pick it up gently.

HOW TO CARE FOR YOUR MONARCH CATERPILLAR

Pick four or five leaves off the milkweed plant and drop them into the jar for the caterpillar to eat. Then, carefully put the caterpillar into the jar and put the lid on. Don't set the jar in a sunny place. Each day have someone watch the caterpillar while you clean its home. Replace the old milkweed leaves with new ones. Then put the caterpillar back inside the jar.

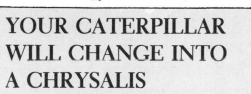

YOUR CATERPILLAR WILL CHANGE INTO A CHRYSALIS

When the caterpillar is full grown, it will hang upside down from the lid of the jar, shed its skin, and form its chrysalis. Don't touch the chrysalis.

THE CHRYSALIS WILL CHANGE INTO YOUR MONARCH BUTTERFLY

In about two weeks, you will be able to see through the chrysalis. It is time for the monarch butterfly to come out. When it does, it will need a few hours for its wings to grow and dry.

HOW TO RELEASE YOUR BUTTERFLY OUTSIDE

A monarch butterfly doesn't want to be a pet. Carefully let it climb out of the jar onto your finger. When it is ready to go, it will fly up into the sky. Or you can leave the opened jar outside in a safe place.

The monarch butterflies that hatch in the spring and early summer only live for a few weeks. The ones that hatch in midsummer are the ones that migrate. They live eight to nine months.

About a hundred million monarchs migrate each year.

Some monarchs fly as high as 2,000 feet.

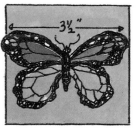

A monarch can have a wing spread of 3½ inches.

In Santa Cruz, California, a monarch butterfly flag is hoisted the day the monarchs arrive. It is flown for six months until the last monarch butterfly leaves for the north.

Pacific Grove, California, calls itself Butterfly Town, U.S.A.

The Monarch Project has volunteers that tag thousands of butterflies to track how fast and how far they fly.

In Mexico there are nature reserves where the monarch butterflies spend the winter.